HEART-SPEAK

Harnessing the Hidden Power of Words

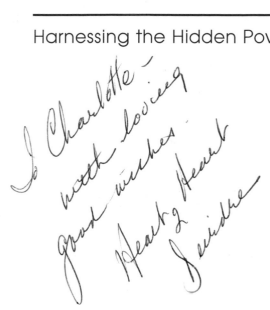

To Charlotte ~
with loving
good wishes.
Hearty Heart
Deirdre

DEIRDRE MORGAN

BALBOA.
PRESS
A DIVISION OF HAY HOUSE

Balboa Press books may be ordered through
booksellers or by contacting:

Balboa Press
A Division of Hay House
1663 Liberty Drive
Bloomington, IN 47403
www.balboapress.com
1 (877) 407-4847

Because of the dynamic nature of the Internet, any web
addresses or links contained in this book may have changed
since publication and may no longer be valid. The views
expressed in this work are solely those of the author and do
not necessarily reflect the views of the publisher, and the
publisher hereby disclaims any responsibility for them.

Any people depicted in stock imagery provided
by Thinkstock are models, and such images are
being used for illustrative purposes only.
Certain stock imagery © Thinkstock.

Print information available on the last page.

ISBN: 978-1-5043-6310-5 (sc)
ISBN: 978-1-5043-6345-7 (e)

Library of Congress Control Number: 2016912082

Balboa Press rev. date: 10/18/2016

CONTENTS

WORDS

GUIDELINES FOR USING YOUR WORDS

TO JOHN – A TRUE WORDSMITH...

Love, Mom

"Be careful when speaking.
You create the world around you
with your words."

Navajo

FOR-WORD

Why do we need to be mindful of how we speak now?

Because the world has changed.
And it will continue to change.
Change is the essence of life.

The past few years has left many people wondering,
"What's going on?"
Often we have felt overwhelmed
or on overdrive with less energy,
tiring more quickly from life's nonstop pace.

For some of us, focusing is even more challenging.
The world seems to be moving faster
and even spinning out of control at times.
It's harder to keep up and to stay clear.

If you feel like this too,
there's a very good explanation.

During the 2012 Winter Solstice,
the new light energy was delivered to our planet.
This energy, which I call The Affirmative Energy Field,
resonates at a different frequency than what we're
used to experiencing.

Because Affirmative Energy is faster,
it creates the challenge for us
to be more flexible
in order to feel more whole and complete.

As a consequence, this Energetic Shift requires us
to approach living differently –
to think, act and speak in a way
that is more in sync with this new frequency.

Interestingly, Affirmative Energy is best processed
and assimilated using our right hemisphere –
or Heart-Centric mind.
No longer can our beliefs, actions and language be
dominated by the left frontal lobe of logic and intellect.

Therefore, the concepts and practices of competition,
divisiveness and intimidation will no longer create
success or happiness.

Instead, we must shift into
a collaborative and compassionate mindset –
a more Heart-Centered way of living that finds
the balance between these competitive hemispheres –
a true melding of Heart and Head
that I call "Heart-Speak".

Now that The Age of Affirmative Energy has arrived
we are tasked with discarding the old patriarchal
paradigm and its Separatist strategies.

We must now recognize that we are One –
united and connected through
our Hearts and Humanity.

It is imperative we celebrate one another;
not tear each other down.
Our goal now is to support our fellow man –
to cooperate rather than compete against him or her.

This is a radically unfamiliar change
and perhaps daunting for most of us.
It requires a near-total reboot
to make this enormous Shift.
The Heart and our emotions have been maligned
and ridiculed for centuries as second-class citizens
to the mighty Intellect.

Well, the game has changed.
Pure intellect will only get you part of the way now.
Success and happiness require a full integration
of the Heart into your approach to life and living.
And yes, even the way you talk.

My sincere wish is that you will awaken your voice,
and speak your intentions clearly
to create a happier life.

All you need to do is –
Use your words wisely!

IN THE BEGINNING...

As written in the Bible,
"In the beginning was the Word..."
And the Word is our beginning!

All words are energy.
All words have meaning.
Words are powerful.

They are physical sound vibrations.
Words shape our emotional connection to life itself.
The words we use form and influence our experience.

We've all heard – "As a man thinketh, so he is."
Well – "As a man speaketh, so he lives."

When you think words, you activate your imagination.
When you speak words, you are aligning yourself
with the Affirmative Energy of The Universe.

Words create Life.
Words can create ease, joy, and fulfillment.

Or they can create anxiety and struggle.
Even failure.

Negative words cause separation
from the Affirmative Energy.
They forge incompatibility – like oil and water.

They originate in the divisive duality
of Right/Wrong... Good/Bad.
This "Separatist Communication" creates
aggression, struggle and disappointment.

Connective, positive words,
those aligned with Affirmative Energy,
are unifying and inclusive.
They are the creative lubricant that generates
effortless "flow" in your life.

Knowing this, we get to choose between Separatist
or Connective Language (Heart-Speak) to link
our intentions to the Affirmative Energy.

Which life will you make happen?

NEW WORLD... NEW WORDS

To interact in the world now,
we are required to shift our perspective.

Technological advances have made our world
"flatter" and smaller.
Our planet is now too interconnected
to remain separated and divisive.

Even though we are individuals, it is now time
to recognize our connection with all living things –
like a single pearl on the strand.
The key is to focus on each other's strengths
rather than our weaknesses.

The "catch" is our logical, left-brain
is terminally stubborn.
Its prime directive, its raison d'etre,
is to make sure we survive.

By design, it favors repeating
the way we have always lived –
same old patterns, habits and routines
that it knows will keep us alive.
So it abhors change.
It campaigns fanatically against change.

Not surprisingly, we are hooked on lists and ledgers.
We are addicted to obeying logic.

We worship linear Power Point presentations.
We admire the clarity of duality –
the stark simplicity of Black and White.
We genuflect at the feet of "the bottom line".

Pure logic no longer works.
It's time to activate our intuitive,
Heart-centered, right-brain process.
Left and right brain are no longer allowed to battle
with each other.
They are required to collaborate
as the Heart is no longer a second-class citizen.

This is best described as -
"Lead with the Heart, follow with Smart."
It's called Connective Communication.
I call it Heart-Speak.

Of course, this new paradigm goes against
all of our training.
We've been brought up to be linear, logical and rational.

However, change demands that we make decisions
in a new way –

> to throw out our history
> let go of intellectual dominance
> move into our hearts
> to no longer believe in pain and
> suffering as the way to grow.

Collaboration and Connective Communication resonate a different energy than Competition and Divisiveness. Now more than ever our words are the key to our finding meaning and happiness.

Therefore, a different language is necessary.
It's essential that our Word-Energy,
the Energy of our Words, be in sync with
this more connected, compassionate way of living.
You can choose the creative route;
or you can choose a chaotic route.

CHOOSE!

SAY WHAT YOU MEAN, MEAN WHAT YOU SAY

We know words are energy
and that our world has changed enormously.
Therefore, our language must evolve accordingly.

Our choice of words can hold us back
by creating dissent and disconnection.
Or, they can free us to create unlimited
prosperity.

As you will soon figure out,
this little book is more than just a practical guide
to refining your language.
These words attune and align your energy
with the new Energetic Principles of Being.
They will change how you talk and how you live.

This is a new world.
The "War of Words" is over.
Intimidation and aggression will no longer be effective.

Using old format language
perpetuates divisiveness, disappointment.
It reinforces the belief that our fellow man
is our adversary, rival and competition.
These outdated beliefs are mired in

"fear, inadequacy and lack".
They are destructive beliefs
promoting limitation and struggle.

Collaboration, compassion and unity
are the new currencies of life.
Trust has replaced fear.
Love has replaced inadequacy.
When you Trust and Love,
you think Abundance
rather than lack.

Do you wish to live a more engaged, authentic life –
a happier and more prosperous existence?

If this is your desire, now is the time to shift
into the language of Heart-Speak –
words that inspire and create greater generosity.
Words that better integrate and align you
with the new Affirmative Energy.
Heart-Speak harnesses the clarity and focus
which are key to your success and happiness.

So...

Old format?
Or New?

WORD TO THE WISE...

WORDS are transformative.
When spoken, they become dynamic sound waves,
beacons of creative, affirmative energy
that transport our intentions.

The Ancients knew this.
They understood that the words they expressed
influenced the process of creating.

For instance, the word "Abracadabra"
is an Aramaic word with roots meaning —
"I create as I speak."

It then evolved into — "I create like the word."
In Hebrew it came to mean —
"It came to pass as spoken."

Sadly, the beautiful truth of this word
has been trivialized and lost over time.

Yet, it still holds the magic of life.

And on some level we each know this.
We know that we are co-creators of our reality.
We know that there is a powerful energy in us –
a Creative Spark!

This book is designed to assist you

in aligning and connecting with the new Energy
that permeates our Universe.

The following pages contain a guide
to assist you in speaking this new language.

I've also included a lexicon of "old format" words
from the Separatist Paradigm of disconnection.
It is time to replace this language
and its unproductive, combative energy.

We use these old words automatically, out of habit.
Unhooking from this antiquated style of thought
and expression takes time.
It will take some practice.

So be gentle with yourself.
There is no benefit to disparaging yourself.
It will keep you feeling "inadequate", lacking.
That's old paradigm.

Stay mindful; keep using the new words.
Practice every day.
Out loud.
Re-frame your thinking.
Set the Field.
Define your Intention.
Delicately re-phrase what you said
when you catch yourself in outdated messaging.

When you make these changes,
you will reshape your vocabulary
to reflect the Heart-based consciousness
of the Affirmative Universe.

Some people call this magical!

And in many ways, it is.

Abracadabra!

Surprised?

Think about it.
What we "want" is usually something we don't have.
We lack.
Want literally means "to lack, to be deficient".

Therefore, when we use the word "want"
we are continuing to reinforce what we don't have
by projecting it into The Affirmative Field.
The Universe can only reflect this same energy.
We are programming poverty consciousness.

And we wonder why things don't change!

What to do?

Precisely define your Intention.
Set the Field with the Affirmative Energy of Abundance.
Use **LIKE, DESIRE, PREFER, CHOOSE** or even **WISH.**

These words make all things probable!

WORRY

We think of WORRY as Caring.
We worry about people and situations.

However, worry is based in doubt,
fear and lack of **TRUST.**
We worry when we think that someone
isn't able to manage.
This creates a negative construct,
a projection of fear.

Worry is a form of torture.
Worry doesn't work.

When we worry,
we send counter-productive energy to the person.
We are really sending them or ourselves,
more to deal with.
All our doubts and fears
are dumped on them
to overcome.
It gets us nowhere.
It just creates stress.

Worry is a drain on everyone.
Worry simply pollutes the Energy Field.
And makes it tougher to move forward and enjoy Life.

Solution?

Stop running ragged on the gerbil wheel of worry.
Remove "Worry" from your vocabulary.

Instead of saying, "I am worried about your trip."
Reframe how you care positively.
Lead with the Heart.
Set the Field with Affirmative Energy.

"I know you will have a good trip."
"Your trip will be great."

Believe it Out Loud.

You can also meditate to prime the Field.
Breathe.
Send them Affirmative Thoughts.
Send them love!
Send them gold Angels!
Give yourself and them a reason to believe.
TRUST.

And when your mind starts to race with doubts,
Breathe and ask yourself –

"Do I really want to do this to myself today?"
Is this real?
Or just a story I am telling myself?

Then redirect your attention to something else.
This creates a Win-Win for everyone!!

"TRY" is the "trickster"
because energetically it anticipates failure.
When you try, you're finished before you've begun.
You're really just "hoping".

Try is a "definite maybe".

Try has too little Heart in it.
It won't get the job done.

Try is not an Intention.
It communicates uncertainty.

It indicates your energy and focus is scattered.
Try undermines belief and determination.

Think Yoda in Star Wars —
"Do or do not. There is no try."

A far more effective word to use is— **CHOOSE.**

Choose resonates Affirmative Energy.
Choose is empowering.
Choose is Heart-Speak.
It is pro-active.
It is focused.

When you choose, it indicates Intention.
You are decisive.
Committed.
"All in!"
It is a completely different energy
and mindset than try.

Other great word choices
to create Affirmative Energy are —
"I'll do my best."
"I'm doing my best."
"I did my best."

Because you are!
At that moment, you're giving Life your best shot.

You do your best.
There is no try.

FAULT

Blame and finding FAULT are not constructive.
Finger-pointing doesn't move a situation forward.

And if you're not solution oriented, what's the point?
Everyone gets stuck in the muddle.
"It's his/your fault..."
"You/he/she made me..."
"You did it to me..."

These are victim statements.
And you've made yourself the victim.
Blame/Shame energy won't work.
Especially now.

Finding fault only pollutes the Energy Field.
It creates defensive resistance.
"Make wrongs" close minds, kill Collaboration.

Solution?

Give everyone a break -
Instead of cross-examination,
begin with self-examination.
Stop finding fault with yourself or others.
Skip playing the blame/shame game.
Instead of demonizing,
Lead with harmonizing.

Change the script – use the word **RESPONSIBLE.**
Instead of saying—
"It's my fault we didn't meet the deadline."
Try re-phrasing it.
"I'm responsible for missing the deadline."

Own your part.
It's your life.
It's on you!

GUILT

Everyone knows what GUILT is.
Everyone knows how it feels.
And it never feels good.

Guilt might work in the short term.
But it comes at a very high price.
One paid in resentment and ultimately disconnection.

Controlling someone with guilt is emotional blackmail.
It's making someone else responsible for your happiness.
Sooner or later, someone tires of the gig.

And we wonder why there's so much divorce?

There is nothing loving about
making a person an indentured servant –
or pulling their strings like a marionette.

Guilt is fear-based.
Fear is subtractive energy.
It is not love.
It makes people feel "less than".

Fear originates in our brains –
from our Head-thinking.
Its primordial purpose was to keep us alive.
Now it simply keeps us from living.

You can recognize "guilt" language
because it's conditional.
It often starts with "If you really love me…"

Guilt-speak creates indebtedness.
And these debts are stored on long lists
that the holder never forgets… or lets you forget.

Does any of this sound fun?
Does any of it create happiness or joy?

Instead of guilt and control, we have another choice.
It may sound corny.
It's called Love.

The Affirmative Energy Field is **LOVE**.
Happiness and success radiate from Heart-thinking.
So dump guilt.

Speak your Truth by loving and respecting yourself.

And see how The Universe responds!

SHOULD

SHOULD is my least favorite word.

It indicates that you are making decisions
based on external considerations.
Put simply —
it's what we think we are "supposed to" do.

And often, your Heart isn't in it.
You don't really care to do it.
Therefore the energy is only half-hearted.
That doesn't create Success.

Should's companions are guilt, obligation and resentment.
Should's roommates are "must" and "have to".
They also excel at creating drama.
Evict them.
Tell them you're just not into them any more.

So what will work?

Stop filtering yourself through someone else's say so.
Instead, Lead with your Heart.
Determine exactly what you desire without Judgment.
Claim your Inner Authority.
Then Set the Field by stating your Intention.

We do this using Affirmative Energy words such as –
CAN, WILL, COULD, and **WOULD.**

Now use your Intention to find a way
to enjoy the task at hand.

Do the things you like to do.
Like the things you "have" to do.

SHOULDA… WOULDA… COULDA!

These three words are the culprits
that warp your mindset.

They are the "sticklers"!
They keep you stuck, anchored in the past.

Stop wasting time.
Skip the regrets.
What's done is done and you're still here.
You did your best at the time,
given what you knew.

How to unhook?

Stop talking with this mindset.
Lose SHOULDA, WOULDA and COULDA
from your vocabulary.

Figure out what you learned;
how the experience made you stronger, wiser.

Ask yourself - Did I give it my best shot?
Did I do everything I knew to do?
If not, remember this going forward.
And Re-frame your Mindset.

When the Shoulda's badger me,

I find this exercise helpful–

BREATHE... Often and deeply.
Find the Awareness of your Breathing.
Say out loud —
"I live and give my best each day.
The Universe supports me fully."
BREATHE.
As you exhale, let your "Shoulda" go.

BUT is a harsh word.
It creates division and divisiveness.

People shut down, stop listening, get defensive.
Creativity and moving forward become a tough sell.
Collaboration and cooperation become even tougher.

A stronger choice?

AND!
It resonates Affirmative Energy.
AND creates and connects.
AND works.
And is Heart-Speak!

Say these sentences out loud --

"I know you think this is best, but I disagree."
"I know you think this is best, and I disagree."

Do you feel the energetic difference?
AND keeps the conversation open and constructive.

You can also use **HOWEVER** or **YET.**
These words create Affirmative Energy.
They are proactive, non judgmental and Collaborative.
They are empowering.

Use 'em!

HOPE is a perversion.

Hope doesn't get the job done.
Hope indicates doubt.
It conveys the energy of insecurity.

Deep down you don't really believe in yourself
or what you're doing.
Energetically, you've given up –
thrown in the towel.

How do we change this Energy?

Instead of "hoping" – **TRUST** and keep going!

Trust is a magnetic Affirmative Word
loaded with Heart.
And you gotta have Heart!
Trust states your Intention.
It sets the Field.

You can also use **BELIEVE.**

Now gently listen inside...

"I hope I get the job."

Versus –

"I trust I got the job."
"I believe I got the job."

Can you feel and hear the difference?
The Universe sure can!

IF indicates doubt and fear are your core thinking.
If implies your Heart is missing in action.

Like "try" and "hope", if doesn't get the job done.
Hypotheticals do not create manifestation.
They lack of conviction and enthusiasm.
You need more Intention and Optimism
to create success.

To activate your Affirmative Energy,
Use the word **WHEN.**
When activates your will, vision and belief.
When is upbeat – filled with ease and joy.
When helps manifest your Heart's desire.

For example:
"When I win the raffle, I'll donate the money."
Not – "If I win the raffle, I'll donate the money."

The energetic difference is remarkable.
When states your Intention clearly.
It Sets the Field.
It creates your future.

So Be Creative.

REMEMBER –
When you don't believe in you, who else can?

EITHER/OR

EITHER/OR is the perfect example
of polarized thinking.
Polarity creates the false Duality that we live in.

Either/Or is not Affirmative Energy.
Duality does not do Connection!
It only creates limitation – obstacles instead of options.

Either/Or is an ultimatum.
Its energy is based in fear and lack.
It is a negative vibration.
Its energy causes waves of friction.

In this new world, the goal is to align your Self
with positive Affirmative Energy.
Our Self thrives on
Connection, Creativity and Inspiration.

For example,
in Duality there's either "hot" or "cold".
That's an Illusion.
A Lie.
Temperature varies.
Your hot can be my cold.
Yet we're both happy.

Either/Or believes that there are only two options –
when in fact there are many.

Recognizing this deception requires a new perception.
Open your mind.
Think outside the box.
Be Creative.

Why allow Either/Or to restrict our ability
to create Options and Solutions?
When we know The Universe is Limitless!

It is time to recognize we are Limitless.

We can have it all.
Because it's All inside us!

DESERVE

DESERVE is the quintessential word to express lack.
Like WANT, it creates a huge energetic void.

Deserve reflects a belief
that you need to justify yourself.
It indicates that "proof of worthiness" is needed.

Nothing could be further from the truth.

You have what you have
because you desired and created it.
You were willing to state your Intention
and Set the Field.
You were committed to giving
what it took to succeed.

Eliminate Deserve from your vocabulary.

Replace it with the Heart-Speak words
LOVE, LIKE or **DESIRE.**
These words resonate with your Heart
and Affirmative Intentions.

Use them—and often!

GUIDELINES FOR USING YOUR WORDS

NOTES:

WHAT YOU PERMIT,
YOU PROMOTE!

This simply means that what you allow in your Life
is your responsibility.
No blame-shame on someone else is acceptable.
Creating and maintaining boundaries
is a function of self-respect and self-worth.

No one makes you do anything.
No one does anything to you unless you allow it.

This is very important to remember
when dealing with Pity-Potters and Time Vampires.
Get clear with yourself.
Their presence in your life is by your consent.

Your emotions are yours.
If emotional upheaval is in your life,
you've put it there.
You've primed The Field for it.
You've endorsed it.
Learn to say, "no".

Option?

Be alert.
Stay conscious!
Define your boundaries.
Stop being the "victim".
Become the victor.
Play Win-Win!

OFF THE PITY POT YET?

We all have moments when we feel sorry for ourselves.
It's human for fear and doubt to take hold sometimes.

But hold on!
We're victimizing ourselves.
We're making ourselves feel inadequate.

If you're on the pot, get off it.
Reframe your outlook.
Find the lesson to be learned.
Then re-Set the Field
by defining your Intention clearly.
Remember: We co-create our Reality
with the Affirmative Field.

We all have people in our lives who are Pity-Potters.
These are the manipulators, Debbie Downers, in our lives.
They are looking to get attention.
These people love being on the pity pot!

It's how they get someone to take responsibility
for their lives by taking care of them.

"Poor me", "lonely me" and "I've been wronged"
are victim statements discharging waves of toxic energy.
Giving advice only hooks you into their drama.

Your best option?

Stop engaging.
Fixing things for Pity-Potters only enables them.
To be a good friend, acknowledge the problem.
"I'm sorry you're going through this."

And then - ask them what they'd like to do about it.
Keep it short.
It's their job to find a solution.
Not yours.

Enabling a Pity-Potter isn't love.
It's a prison sentence.

PROBLEM SOLVER

"Problem solvers" always need problems.
They do this to define themselves, feel important.

Their identity and self-worth
are based in being the hero or savior.
It's an ongoing, never changing process
outsourced in other people and situations.

The Problem Solver escalates the problem.
This elevates their value.
Simple and easy is not part of their vocabulary.
It doesn't provide enough ROI - "Return On Involvement".
They seek an "ego payout" more than a Solution.

An attitude adjustment is needed.
So become a SOLUTION MAKER.

Solution Makers are in the creative, heart-based mindset.
They see problems as opportunities.
Optimism, humor and confidence are their BFF.

Instead of playing Debbie Downer,
they opt for "How do I make this work?"

In these new times, it's about sourcing from within.
Just dig a little deeper,
the Solutions are waiting for you.

Feeling good with yourself,
not needing to prove anything
is easy when you believe
Everything's inside you.

So... how do you make it work for you?

YOU DON'T
HAVE THE VOTE!

Want someone to change, be different?
Want to change how they think, do things?

Guess what?

You don't have the vote!

Even if you're "right",
it's not your life.
People aren't here to meet your needs
or expectations.
They're here to meet their own.

So - stop depending on them
for your happiness and well being.
Start meeting your own needs.

How about loving yourself?

IF YOU FEAR IT, DO IT!

"If you fear it, do it!" -- Thank you, Eleanor Roosevelt.
Fear indicates self-doubt.
It minimizes confidence.

Are you letting fear
run some area of your life?

What's to be afraid of?
What are you really afraid of?

Whatever it is, take action.

We don't shed fear by thinking our way out of it.
Fear thrives on "paralysis from analysis".
Your head won't lead you out of fear.
Only your Heart can do that.

We must leave our "comfort zone"
no matter how scary.
So take Heart.
Be courageous!

Define your Intention.
Set the Field.
Taking action heals the fear.
Taking action creates confidence.

That's a success story!

LEAD WITH THE HEART, FOLLOW WITH SMART

"Lead with the Heart, follow with Smart"
is self-explanatory.

Listen to your Heart.
What energizes you?
Makes you feel good inside?

Be imaginative.
Be playful.

Then be Smart –
Use common sense
to support your dream
and get the project done.

Remember: Right and Left brain
need to work together to collaborate.

Now you've Set the Field for optimal success.
Go for the Gold!

TALKING WITH

Talking To and Talking At are old format.

It's authoritarian.
It is considered condescending
because it's pontificating.
Who wants to listen to that?

There is no "We".
No exchange.
It is subtractive energy.
It is not Connective, Heart-Speak language.
And in these new times,
Connection is a Commandment.

Instead, talk WITH people.
Engage them.
Ask them questions.
"What do you think about..."
"What's your opinion about..."

With builds rapport.
It's easier to understand different points of view.
It's easier to negotiate, to get things done.

Someone once said –

"If you want to go quickly, go it alone.
If you want to go far, go with others."

WIN – WIN

Win-Win is Heart-Speak!
Win-Win is two-way communication.
It's not new – it's been around a long time now.

This is definitely a "feel good" approach to conversations
that are potentially confrontational.
More importantly, Win-Win is solution oriented.

Here are the rules to Win-Win—

1. Never start with the word "you".
    "You make me…"
    "You did this to me…"
    "It's your fault that…"
    These are "make wrong" statements.
    They create divisiveness.
    When you make people "wrong" -
    they get defensive.
    They shut down and stop listening.
    What does that solve?

2. Win-Win!
    Use "I" statements.
    "I" statements empower everyone.
    "I'm upset that…"
    "I get annoyed when…"
    You aren't victimizing yourself,
    or villainizing someone else.

Then state what's bothering you.

3. ASK the other person for a solution.
    Questions create collaboration.
    People like to have input.
    Being creatively involved empowers them.

4. Win-Win!
    If they give a great solution, go with it.
    If they answer: "I don't know."
    Make your suggestion.

5. If they give a solution that won't work –
    Suggest yours <u>in question form</u>.

6. Whatever is decided, agree to a trial run.

Win-Win is an opportunity to be proactive and creative.
Everyone feels invested in the Solution.
Everyone comes out a winner!

BELIEVING OUT LOUD

We create from the subconscious
not the conscious mind.
This is why our Word-Energy is so important.
It creates our Intention and Sets the Field.

One of the best ways to materialize your dreams
is to Believe and Imagine living it!
Some people call this – "Fake it 'til you make it."
I call it Believing Out Loud.

Believing Out Loud activates the subconscious.
It infuses it with Affirmative Energy.
Now, speak with clear Intention.
This confirms your desired Reality.

"I am healed, whole and 100% healthy."

This Sets the Field.
It promotes Creation.
The Universe can then manifest your Intention.

This makes for a much easier process.
And a more enjoyable one!

SOUL IN GROWTH

This is a great phrase to get you to stop "Judging".

Judging is not additive energy.
It is subtractive energy.
It can be addictive though!
When you don your black robes
and wield your gavel,
does this truly empower you?
Subtractive energy makes everyone feel smaller.

Just because we don't like or understand
what someone is doing, let them be!
Live and Let Love.
It's their growth and journey.

We're all doing the best we can.
You don't/can't know the level of doubts and fears
they're holding inside.
You have your own "stuff" to deal with.
Does being judged feel good to you?

Remember, our job is to build each other up.
Not tear one another down.
You can ask if they want your opinion.
Otherwise, don't give it.
Button it!

Will Rogers once said,
"Never miss a good chance to shut up."

KISS THE JOY!

"Kiss the Joy" means to appreciate.
Appreciation means to enlarge, to expand.
It's a form of investment – in yourself.

It's similar to a savings account.
What you put in - comes back with interest.
It depends on how much Heart you've expressed.
It's a natural organic process.

When we value who we are
and the good things we have in our life,
we open ourselves to greater opportunities.

Without Appreciation, life stays small.

Kissing the Joy acknowledges life with enthusiasm.
Do you acknowledge these "feel good" times
to yourself, others?
Do you see the cups half-full?
Or overflowing?

Express Appreciation by smiling, laughing
and hugging often.
It's infectious!
Life gets bigger!

So – why not enjoy?

HONOR THE
SACRED WITHIN

Remember who you are!

At essence, you are an Infinite Being,
Unlimited in your potential
as Abundant Energy and Flow.

You are whole, complete.
You lack for nothing!

Acknowledge this often.
Each day Meditate and Affirm –

"I AM AN INFINITE BEING, LOVING AND LOVED,
HEALTHY, VITAL, DYNAMIC AND ABUNDANT!"

Always was.
Always will be.

All Ways.

ARE YOU THE REAL DEAL?

Since the new energy downloads arrived in late 2012,
the goal we each now share is finding our Authentic Selves.
We are tasked with living our Truth.
Finding our Passion.
Living from our Hearts.
Being the Real Deal.

For some this will be easy.
For others it will be taxing.

Either way, we have no vote in the matter.
The Affirmative Universe now requires this change.

So find yourself.
Discover again what thrills you,
What lightens your energy?
What inspires you?
What makes you giggle and laugh?

Find your Joy.
And in that Joy, experience . . .
Peace.
Unity.
Connection.
Happiness.
Love.

Heart-Speak is how we express ourselves.
How we remember our Authentic Self.
And how we manifest change and experience happiness.

Remember - the sounds we voice create an energetic wave,
the first physical manifestation of our Heart's Desire.

Words matter.
Will you speak from your Heart?

THE FINAL WORD

Okay – so now you are aware that...

Words reflect your beliefs about yourself and the world.
Words affect the Affirmative Energy around us.

How we talk to ourselves and with each other,
can give us a greater sense of wholeness and wellbeing.
This Abundance is our natural God-given state.
It is our birthright.
On some level, you already know this.

Using the Heart-Speak words
of Connection and Empowerment in this book,
allows you to accept and connect more deeply
with your Creative Source,
your own spark of Divinity.

The time has arrived to express more Love.
Life is about loving yourself.
It begins inside us.
Word + "L" for Love = your World.

Now be the change in the Word!
Heart-Speak!

Printed in the United States
By Bookmasters